THE ENTOURAGE

The People Behind the Athlete

By Chrös McDougall

SportsZone
An Imprint of Abdo Publishing
abdobooks.com

abdobooks.com

Published by Abdo Publishing, a division of ABDO, PO Box 398166, Minneapolis, Minnesota 55439.

Printed in the United States of America, North Mankato, Minnesota.
102025
012026

THIS BOOK CONTAINS RECYCLED MATERIALS

Cover Photo: Dominique Oliveto/Getty Images for Klutch Sports Group 2019 All Star Weekend/Getty Images Entertainment/Getty Images
Interior Photos: Gregory Shamus/Getty Images Sport/Getty Images, 1, 42–43; Andy Devlin/National Hockey League/Getty Images, 3, 21; Mike Ehrmann/Getty Images Sport/Getty Images, 4–5, 47; Kristina Bumphrey/Sportico/Getty Images, 7; Cliff Welch/Icon Sportswire/Getty Images, 8; Michael Reaves/Getty Images Sport/Getty Images, 11; Brian Babineau/National Hockey League/Getty Images, 12–13; Focus On Sport/Getty Images Sport/Getty Images, 15; Bettmann/Getty Images, 16; Jamie Squire/Allsport/Getty Images Sport/Getty Images, 18; Bob Levey/Getty Images Sport/Getty Images, 22, 36; Vaughn Ridley/Getty Images Sport/Getty Images, 24–25; Julia Mikhaylova/Shutterstock Images, 26; Al Bello/Getty Images Sport/Getty Images, 28–29; Ronald Martinez/Getty Images Sport/Getty Images, 30; Xavier Laine/Getty Images Sport/Getty Images, 33, 45; Ron Jenkins/Getty Images Sport/Getty Images, 34–35; Lisa Lake/Getty Images for Prime Video/Getty Images Entertainment/Getty Images, 38; Nick Wosika/Icon Sportswire/Getty Images, 41

Editor: Christa Kelly
Series Designer: Maggie Villaume

Library of Congress Control Number: 2025939130

Publisher's Cataloging-in-Publication Data

Names: McDougall, Chrös, author.
Title: The entourage: the people behind the athlete / by Chrös McDougall
Description: Minneapolis, Minnesota: Abdo Publishing, 2026 | Series: The business of sports | Includes online resources and index.
Identifiers: ISBN 9781098298258 (lib. bdg.) | ISBN 9798384932055 (ebook)
Subjects: LCSH: Sports--Juvenile literature. | Social groups--Juvenile literature. | Groupies--Juvenile literature. | Friends and associates--Juvenile literature. | Professional staff--Juvenile literature. | Sports in popular culture--Juvenile literature.
Classification: DDC 306.4830--dc23

TABLE OF CONTENTS

BUCCANEERS
12

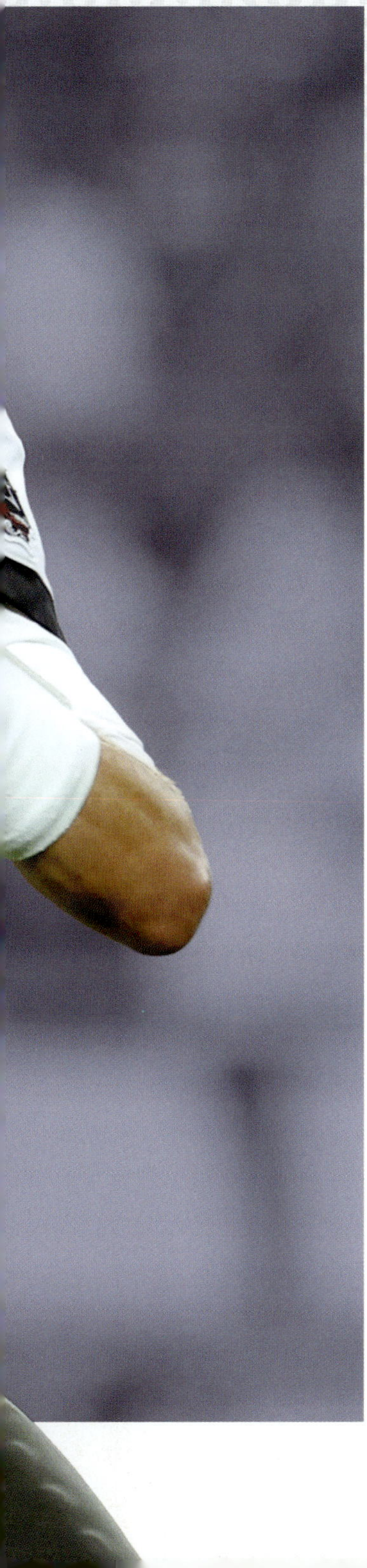

CHAPTER ONE

THE TEAM BEHIND TOM

The sports world celebrated Tom Brady on February 1, 2022. The superstar quarterback had played 22 National Football League (NFL) seasons. During that time, he'd won a record seven Super Bowl championships with the New England Patriots and Tampa Bay Buccaneers. Now, at age 44, he was retiring from the sport. "I have loved my NFL career," Brady wrote announcing his decision, "and now it is time to focus my time and energy on other things that require my attention."

Brady's retirement lasted all of 41 days. On March 13, Brady called Gilad Haas. Haas managed Brady's social media. Brady told Haas he was having second thoughts about retirement. He planned to announce his comeback that day. When a famous athlete like Brady makes news,

Tom Brady earned $30 million in 2022, bringing his career earnings to nearly $330 million.

there's often a team of helpers behind it. That's where Haas came in.

Building His Team

Brady began his NFL career in 2000. Within five years, he had led the Patriots to three Super Bowl titles. Around this same time, social media was taking off. Facebook, Twitter, Instagram, and Snapchat were all founded between 2004 and 2011.

Ben Rawitz, who was working as Brady's personal assistant, managed the quarterback's online presence. Rawitz's brother, Jeff Fine, began helping too. Eventually, Haas joined them. In 2017, the three partnered with Brady to create a company called Shadow Lion.

The company initially focused on creating posts for Brady's social media. Before long, it took on other roles as well. Shadow Lion partnered with brands on marketing campaigns. It created original content, such as videos and podcasts. The company also worked with other athletes and companies. By 2023, Shadow Lion had more than a dozen employees and was still growing. But even as the company grew, Brady's online presence remained one of its top priorities.

Shadow Lion had played a big role in crafting Brady's initial retirement announcement. Brady had wanted his message to honor those who had been part of his football journey,

Before working with Brady, Gilad Haas, *pictured*, worked for Patriots wide receiver Julian Edelman.

including his teammates, coaches, and family. His partners at Shadow Lion used their expertise to craft the perfect announcement video.

Now, just a few weeks later, Brady was ready to make another big announcement. Haas, Shadow Lion's managing director, was at a Boston Celtics basketball game when Brady called. Brady told Haas he wanted to announce his return to the Buccaneers in about 30 minutes. They discussed what Brady would say. They selected two pictures to accompany the post. One showed Brady lined up before a play with his Buccaneers teammates. The other showed Brady's family. Half an hour later, the announcement hit social media.

With seven Super Bowl rings and five Super Bowl MVP Awards, Brady is considered one of the greatest football players of all time.

"These past two months I have realized my place is still on the field and not in the stands," Brady said in his Instagram post. "I'm coming back for my 23rd season in Tampa. We have unfinished business."

Rise of the Entourage

People have been taking part in sports since ancient times. But sports became a business during the mid-1800s. Organizers realized there was money to be made selling tickets to watch sporting events. Athletes, in turn, demanded compensation for attracting fans to games.

Over the years, sports began bringing in more and more money. The rise of athlete endorsements and cable TV during the 1980s and 1990s led to huge increases in athlete pay. Today, the most successful athletes earn tens of millions of dollars each year.

A professional athlete's top priority is succeeding in competition. But that isn't an athlete's only responsibility. Sports are businesses. Negotiating contracts, managing money, and maintaining an online presence are just a few of the things athletes must now do on the business side. Increasingly, athletes are surrounding themselves with people who can help manage these extra responsibilities.

Often, an athlete's entourage includes family and friends. They can help keep the athlete grounded. However, with so much money involved, athletes often need to surround themselves with professionals as well. Sports agents represent athletes in business decisions, such as contract negotiations. Accountants and business managers help athletes manage their money. Personal assistants and managers can organize an athlete's various commitments. Athletes might also choose to work with personal chefs, dieticians, trainers, and other professionals to help maintain their physical peak.

Inside Brady's Brand

For many years, fans heard from athletes primarily in the press. Reporters from newspapers and TV stations interviewed athletes. Then the reporters shared the athletes' responses in their stories. This traditional media model remains an important way for fans to learn about their favorite teams and athletes. However, the rise of social media has given athletes more opportunities to communicate directly with fans. Creating a strong social media presence can also help an athlete gain exposure. This can lead to endorsements and other opportunities to earn money.

Brady was among the athletes who embraced this new approach. In 2013, when Fine was still in college, he convinced Brady to create his own social media accounts. At the time, many fans knew Brady only as a serious and competitive quarterback. Through his social media, Brady was able to show a more lighthearted side of himself. With the internet-savvy Fine running the accounts, fans got to see Brady's values and sense of humor.

Haas brought additional expertise to the group. Haas began by making videos for one of Brady's teammates. Once the group formed Shadow Lion, they took on more ambitious projects. In 2018, they helped produce *Tom vs Time*. The six-part docuseries follows Brady's life off the

PUBLIC RELATIONS

Requests to talk to an athlete are often fielded by the athlete's team or agent. But some athletes have public relations (PR) representatives to handle these requests. PR reps coordinate interviews. They might also look for opportunities to get their clients in the news. They help manage an athlete's reputation by encouraging positive and accurate coverage. In addition, PR reps can help navigate communication during a crisis.

field, giving insight into who he is as a person. This exposure helped reinforce Brady as one of the most important athletes of his era.

Looking back on this time, Brady recalled being reluctant to share his personal life with the world. He had considered himself to be a private person. He wasn't sure if he wanted to share so much about his life. Working with Shadow Lion changed his views. The company helped him share his story in a way "that feels right and true to who I am," he said. That approach has helped him connect with more fans.

Brady retired from football for good after the 2023 season. However, he still has a huge following. In 2025, Brady had 15.2 million followers on Instagram, plus another 4.9 million on Facebook and 3 million on X (formerly Twitter). With the help of Shadow Lion, Brady remains one of the most famous figures in all of sports.

After Brady's retirement from the NFL, he signed a 10-year, $375 million deal to join Fox Sports' broadcast team.

SKIP
29
KARBON-X
OILERS
CCM

CHAPTER TWO

SPORTS AGENTS

By 2024, Leon Draisaitl had played 10 seasons in the National Hockey League (NHL), all with the Edmonton Oilers. The German-born center was an elite playmaker. He'd already enjoyed three 50-goal seasons. In one of them, he won the Hart Memorial Trophy. This award is given out every year to the most valuable player in the NHL. In June 2024, Draisaitl helped bring the Oilers within one win of a Stanley Cup championship. Soon after, the team called Draisaitl's agents, Mike Liut and Andy Scott.

At 28 years old, Draisaitl was in the prime of his career. He still had one year remaining on his contract. However, if the Oilers let that deal expire, Draisaitl would be free to sign with any team. Edmonton general manager Stan Bowman didn't want to risk losing his star.

Edmonton Oilers superstar Leon Draisaitl made $8 million during the 2023–24 season.

Draisaitl didn't want to leave Edmonton either. The team had taken him third overall in the 2014 draft. He had thrived there ever since. Draisaitl directed Liut and Scott to negotiate an extension with the Oilers.

Negotiating a contract is serious work. For an athlete like Draisaitl, a contract is worth millions of dollars. Contracts are also legal documents. Agents are experts at handling these contracts in ways that most athletes aren't.

Agents can also be useful when negotiations become contentious. Both the player and the team have their own interests. An agent advocates for their client. At the same time, the agent can shield the athlete from potentially hurtful feedback.

Draisaitl told his agents what he hoped to get from a new contract. He also set a timeline. If he was going to re-up with Edmonton early, the deal had to be complete before training camp for the 2024–25 season. With that, Liut and Scott set out to make a deal.

Handling the Business

Professional sports leagues bring in billions of dollars each year. While athletes still play for the love of the game, they want to be paid fairly. Athletes also increasingly have opportunities to make money through endorsements or

Before Mike Liut was an agent, he was a professional hockey goalie.

LOUISVILLE
LOUISVILLE
Cooper
DURA-SOFT
DURA-SOFT

Red Grange played for the Chicago Bears in 1925 and again from 1929 to 1934.

other business endeavors. Today's stars often turn to various professionals to help manage the business side of their careers.

In the 1920s, University of Illinois football player Red Grange became the first athlete to hire an agent. Grange was a skilled running back, and his incredible speed and long runs captivated fans around the nation. Teams in the NFL wanted to sign Grange. However, the league paid players only $100 to $200 per game.

C. C. Pyle believed Grange was worth more than that. He had met Grange while managing a movie theater. In 1925, he convinced the player to let him negotiate a contract with the NFL's Chicago Bears. With Pyle's help, Grange signed a contract that guaranteed him at least $3,000 per game.

Despite Pyle's success, sports agents remained rare. In the 1950s, agents began taking on larger roles in getting athletes endorsements. But for many years, teams resisted working with agents. The teams wanted to maintain their power. At the time, they had a lot of control over their players. Once a player signed a contract with a team, the player could never sign with another team. This meant players had limited leverage in negotiating contracts. If a player didn't like what their team was offering, their only other option was to not play.

In 1976, Major League Baseball (MLB) players won the right to free agency. Now players whose contracts ended could sign with a different team. Eventually, other leagues followed. Meanwhile, sports were becoming increasingly lucrative businesses. These factors led to an increase in sports agents and, in turn, higher salaries for athletes.

In 1979, pitcher Nolan Ryan became the first baseball player to earn $1 million per season. By 2001, shortstop

During Alex Rodriguez's 22-season career, he played for the Seattle Mariners, Texas Rangers, and New York Yankees.

Alex Rodriguez was making more than $25 million per season. And 25 years later, some baseball players were making twice that.

Agents are best known for negotiating contracts and other business deals. But modern agents also do much more. College football players enter the NFL through the league's draft. Their agents often arrange special training to help the players prepare. Agents can also help clients manage their finances. They can even assist their clients with public relations, marketing, and legal disputes.

Agents have traditionally been athletes' primary representatives. But some athletes now hire multiple people to manage their business interests. Some hire accountants who specialize in working with athletes. These accountants know how to navigate athletes' complex taxes.

Many athletes invest their earnings. However, athletes are busy and often don't have expertise in business. Business managers can help them oversee their investments.

Many athletes also hire publicists. Publicity is increasingly valuable. A publicist can help an athlete get in the news. Public relations and marketing professionals play similar roles in managing an athlete's image.

GOING SOLO

Not all professional athletes use agents. Baltimore Ravens quarterback Lamar Jackson represents himself in business negotiations. In 2023, he signed a new contract that paid him $53 million per year. That made him the NFL's highest-paid player. However, players like Jackson have become an exception. Most employ agents.

Sealing the Deal

Before meeting with the Oilers, Liut and Scott needed to determine what kind of deal they wanted for Draisaitl.

They looked at contracts for other star players. They considered the league's salary cap and how it might change in the coming years. The agents also thought about the length of Draisaitl's contract. A shorter contract might allow Draisaitl to sign another contract for an even higher salary. But a longer contract would guarantee him a lot of money.

Meanwhile, the Oilers held similar conversations. If the team paid Draisaitl too much, it wouldn't have enough money to sign other star players. If it signed him for too long, Draisaitl might lose some of his abilities toward the end of his contract.

Ultimately, both sides had the same goal. They wanted Draisaitl to renew his contract with the Oilers. Now they had to negotiate a deal to make that happen.

Liut and Scott began meeting with Bowman and the Oilers' president of hockey operations, Jeff Jackson, on August 1. Each side presented their case. Then they worked to find common ground. Once they'd agreed on a framework, Draisaitl's agents met with their client to review his options.

Draisaitl's agents explained that he might be able to sign an even bigger contract if he waited until he was a free agent the next summer. However, that could be a gamble. If Draisaitl didn't sign and suffered a career-ending injury that season, he might miss out on millions. Ultimately, Draisaitl decided not to wait. He was happy in Edmonton. He believed he could

After signing his new contract, Draisaitl said he wanted to be an Oiler for life.

29
play alberta
OILERS
WARRIOR

win there. And he liked the idea of playing his entire career in northern Alberta. On September 3, 2024, Draisaitl signed a contract worth $112 million over eight years. With an average salary of $14 million per season, he became the highest-paid player in NHL history.

Scott Boras has represented MLB stars such as Alex Rodriguez, Bryce Harper, and Corey Seager.

CASE STUDY

SCOTT BORAS

Scott Boras played baseball in college. Later, he moved on to the minor leagues. However, he didn't make much of an impact on the sport until he became an agent.

After attending law school and working at a firm for a few years, Boras became a sports agent. He has since developed a reputation as one of baseball's toughest negotiators. He refuses to budge on what he believes his clients are worth. This approach has helped him attract some of baseball's biggest stars.

Boras became the first baseball agent to negotiate a $50 million contract. Later his clients signed the first $100 million and $200 million contracts too. Following the 2019 season, Boras's clients signed contracts worth a total of more than $1 billion.

Boras's biggest deal came after the 2024 season. Outfielder Juan Soto had proven to be one of baseball's most dangerous hitters. And at 26 years old, he was still in the prime of his career. Every team wanted him. Many thought he would return to the New York Yankees. Instead, he joined the crosstown New York Mets. In December 2024, Boras negotiated a 15-year contract for Soto worth $765 million. At the time of signing, it was the largest contract in sports history.

STARR

CHAPTER THREE

PEAK PERFORMERS

Professional baseball players work unusual hours. Games typically start around 7 p.m. But players arrive at the ballpark several hours earlier to begin preparing. The game itself usually lasts more than 2.5 hours. By the time players have showered, spoken to the press, and collected their things, they might not leave until well after 11 p.m. Over the course of a 162-game season, this schedule can make it hard for athletes to maintain healthy eating habits.

Alex Baker is an accomplished chef from New York City. Over the past few years, local MLB players have been hiring her as a private chef. Because of the players' schedules, Baker typically cooks in the morning. She might show up at a player's home at 7 a.m. and cook for three or four hours. When she leaves, the player often has

Baseball has the longest season of the major North American professional sports leagues.

When Alex Baker cooks for athletes, she makes foods with healthy fats and lean protein.

multiple meals to eat. And Baker's food isn't just delicious. It's also nutritious.

"They're hiring me because I know what they're supposed to eat," Baker said. "They don't want to have to think about it. I just avoid things that I know are not healthy or not good for them."

Hiring a private chef like Baker is expensive. A family of five that needs three meals is likely to pay Baker at least $500 per day. And that doesn't include the cost of the food. But for many athletes, the cost of a private chef is well worth it.

"People are starting to realize food as medicine or food as fuel, and it's the same in sports," Baker said. "Some of the athletes I've cooked for have talked about how much better they feel now that they are eating healthy because of their chef."

Building the Body

An athlete's body is their livelihood. Whether they need speed, strength, precision, or all three, athletes need to stay in peak physical condition. This means focusing on fitness, skill development, and recovery, even during the offseason. Increasingly, athletes are also focusing on their mental health and its impact on performance. In each area, experienced professionals can help athletes stay at their best.

Teams in the biggest sports leagues often have staff members in charge of maintaining their athletes' health. In 2018, the Tampa Bay Buccaneers football team experienced a major increase in injuries. To combat this, the team hired a director of athlete performance. He worked with colleagues who were experts in areas such as strength, conditioning, nutrition, and medicine. They studied each player and reviewed the best practices in sports science. Then they used what they learned to help the players stay fit and healthy.

In other cases, athletes hire their own private experts. At 6 feet, 2 inches tall and 247 pounds, Derrick Henry is one of the NFL's biggest running backs. Using his amazing size and strength, Henry bulldozed his way to 2,027 rushing yards in 2020. That made him only the eighth running back to break the 2,000-yard mark. But running back is a demanding position. Henry knew that NFL running backs often don't have long careers.

In 2024, Henry turned 30. That's usually an age when running backs start to slow down. Instead, Henry had one of his best seasons, racking up 1,921 yards. After that, the Baltimore Ravens signed him to a two-year extension worth $30 million.

Henry's longevity is no fluke. He reportedly spends $240,000 each year on "body maintenance." This includes a personal chef. During the offseason, he trains twice a day at a local gym. Henry also invests a lot in recovery, including working with a massage therapist. "He does everything right," former teammate Ben Jones said.

Basketball is another demanding sport. Forward LeBron James turned 40 in December 2024. Yet even in his 22nd National Basketball Association (NBA) season, he

Derrick Henry played for the Tennessee Titans for eight seasons before signing with the Baltimore Ravens in 2024.

OAKLEY
RAVENS
22

LeBron James is the NBA's all-time leading scorer.

remained one of the league's top players. The Los Angeles Lakers star averaged 24.4 points, 7.8 rebounds, and 8.2 assists per game.

This kind of success takes hard work. One of James's business partners once claimed that the player spent $1.5 million per year taking care of his body. James disputed that number. But he said, “I do invest in my body for sure.” James reportedly hires personal chefs, trainers, massage therapists, and other professionals.

Mental Health Matters

Simone Biles rolled out of bed on July 30, 2024, and knew what she had to do. The American gymnast was in Paris, France, to compete at the Olympic Games. But first, she had a session with her therapist.

Athletes face unique challenges. They must perform at a high level, often in front of large crowds. In individual sports, an athlete has no one to shield them if they’re struggling.

In some cases, such as the Olympics, an athlete might have been dreaming of competing on that stage for years. Suddenly being in that moment can become overwhelming. Therapists and sports psychologists specialize in helping athletes cope with these challenges. “I honestly don’t know how you could do it without a sport psychologist,” said Team USA cyclist Lily Williams.

SKATE ON

Growing up, Dawn Braid was one of Canada’s best figure skaters. In 2005, she started sharing her expert skating techniques with NHL players as a skating coach. Having elite skating ability is increasingly important in hockey. Braid has worked with many of the NHL’s top stars including John Tavares and Matthew Tkachuk.

By the Paris Olympics, 27-year-old Biles had already enjoyed a groundbreaking gymnastics career. She was the sport's most decorated athlete, male or female. In Paris, Biles made her mental health a priority.

At the previous Olympics in 2021, Biles had struggled mentally. Her family is her main support system. But due to the COVID-19 pandemic, they were not allowed to attend the Games in Tokyo, Japan. Biles began to feel weighed down by the pressure on her.

Then, in the team final, she experienced the "twisties." This dangerous condition is when a gymnast's mind feels out of sync with their body. Biles ended up withdrawing from five of her six finals in Tokyo. She didn't know if she'd ever compete again.

With the help of her therapist, Biles learned to manage her mental health. In the past, few athletes talked openly about mental health. Biles is one of the athletes who have changed that in recent years. Biles said that regular therapy sessions helped her "feel a lot more free." She added, "Physically and mentally, I feel better."

Biles kept up her therapy sessions while in Paris. On the morning of July 30, she told her therapist she was feeling "calm and ready." A few hours later, she led the US team to a gold medal. She left Paris with three gold medals and a silver.

Despite suffering from the twisties, Simone Biles won a bronze medal on the balance beam at the 2021 Olympics in Tokyo, Japan.

USA
TOKYO 2

BEARS
ONE
XII
8

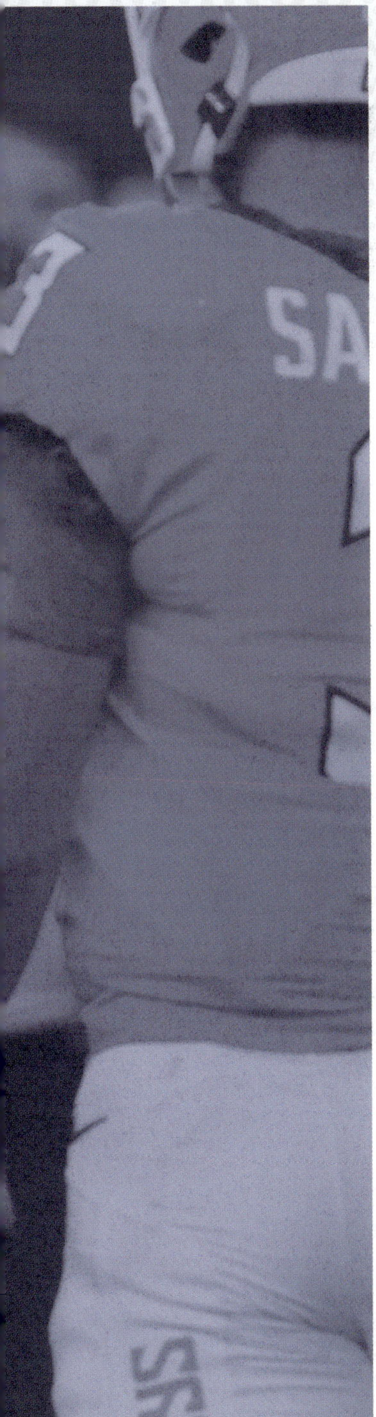

CHAPTER FOUR

BEYOND THE GAME

Baylor University safety Jalen Pitre made plays all over the field in 2021. The Big 12 Conference named him its Defensive Player of the Year. A few months later, the Houston Texans picked Pitre in the second round of the NFL Draft. The 23-year-old signed a four-year contract that would pay him $8.9 million. Then he moved back in with his parents.

Pitre decided to live with his parents after looking for houses online. He had never owned a home before. The ones he was looking at cost upward of $10,000 per month. Spending that much on a house didn't make sense to Pitre at that stage in life. Meanwhile, his parents still lived in his childhood home just 20 minutes from the Texans' stadium. Pitre decided that living with them would help him save money and stay grounded.

Safety Jalen Pitre helped Baylor win the 2021 Big 12 Conference championship.

Pitre recorded 147 tackles during his rookie season with the Houston Texans in 2022.

Being a pro athlete can be exciting and fun. But it also requires hard work. Athletes face a lot of pressure. Suddenly, people around the world know who they are. In the biggest sports leagues, new players often become millionaires overnight. This can be life-changing money for their families. But athletes know that their success depends on their performance. If they play poorly and make bad financial decisions, they could lose it all.

Living with his parents helped Pitre during his transition to NFL fame. When the season started, his days began at 5 a.m. After long hours at practice, he returned home to eat dinner with his parents. Being with his family had always been a break from his intense football responsibilities. That was no different as an NFL rookie.

"It calms my nerves a lot," Pitre said. "I just come home and chill like it's high school, it's no pressure. Not many questions about football stuff."

The setup worked well for Pitre. He ended up starting all 17 games for the Texans during his first season. He even got votes for the NFL's Defensive Rookie of the Year Award.

Managing the Home

It's rare for athletes to move back in with their parents when they start their professional careers. But establishing support systems as part of their entourage is important for young athletes. For young athletes, that can mean living with trusted family and friends. These people knew the athlete before the athlete was rich and famous. They can help keep the athlete grounded and protected.

Longtime NFL star Jason Kelce, *left*, married his wife, Kylie, *right*, in 2018.

As athletes get older, their needs often change. They may eventually get married and have kids of their own. Yet their careers are still demanding. Travel is a regular part of life for professional athletes. That means they can't always be at home with their families.

Football player Jason Kelce played 13 seasons for the Philadelphia Eagles. During that time, he developed into one of the NFL's elite centers. He also became a popular podcast host alongside his brother, fellow NFL star Travis Kelce. Meanwhile, he and his wife, Kylie, raised three daughters. They welcomed a fourth daughter in 2025 after Jason retired. Because of his commitments, Jason relied on Kylie to do a lot of the work around the home.

"I think it's no coincidence I have enjoyed the best years of my career with Kylie by my side," Jason said when he retired in March 2024. "Every accolade I have ever received has come with her in my life."

In many cases, parents can't do everything on their own. That became true for the Kelces. Over the years, Kylie became a field hockey coach and a supporter of the Eagles Autism Foundation. At one point, her podcast was the top-ranked show in the United States. To manage everything, the family needed a childcare team to help watch their kids.

In addition to childcare, professional athletes might need to hire other helpers. A housekeeper can clean and keep the home in order. If an athlete has multiple properties, an estate manager can oversee them when the athlete is away. Personal assistants manage an athlete's schedule and help keep track of the athlete's commitments. Hiring a driver can also be a big help. Instead of focusing on driving, the athlete can use that time to get other work done or relax.

Some athletes even hire personal stylists. These people keep athletes looking their best. Jasmine Caccamo is a personal stylist. Athletes such as soccer star Alex Morgan and skiing champion Mikaela Shiffrin have hired Caccamo to help them look sharp even outside of their competitions.

LOOKING FLY

Several members of the US men's soccer team play professionally in Europe. It can be difficult to find a barber they trust in their new country. So some national team players began flying in a personal barber to their training camps. They knew this barber could cut their hair just how they liked it. That, for them, was worth the cost.

Staying Safe

Basketball player Caitlin Clark rose to superstardom while in college. She dominated the court at the University of Iowa and became one of the most famous college basketball players in the nation. Eventually the smooth-shooting Clark put up more points than any college player before her, man or woman. Along the way, huge crowds followed the Hawkeyes around, hoping to get a glimpse of the famous player.

Most of the fan support was positive. However, all the attention had some downsides too. Late one night after a game, two men approached Clark at her car. It turned out they just wanted her autograph. But the experience spooked Clark and her family.

After that, Clark began working with a private security guard. She continued to hire security after being drafted to the Women's National Basketball Association's Indiana Fever

Caitlin Clark scored 3,951 points during her college career at Iowa from 2020 to 2024.

in 2024. "Steve follows me around, he's over there in the corner," Clark joked during training camp. "Don't mess with Steve."

Clark is hardly alone in having personal security. Many professional athletes are famous celebrities. People want to be close to the athletes. Sometimes these people can become obsessive. Others see athletes as easy targets to rob.

The rise of sports betting has also led to an increase in threats toward athletes. Athletes need to prioritize their safety. Many leagues and teams now provide security for players, especially when they're traveling. But individual athletes are increasingly protecting themselves with private security too.

Professional athletes have extraordinary lives. They play games for a living. They get to perform in front of adoring crowds. And in some cases, they earn millions of dollars for doing it. At the end of the day, though, athletes are like other working people. They have families, homes, and responsibilities. They have dreams and aspirations. They also must overcome stress and hardships. A trusted entourage can help an athlete navigate this life and chase their dreams.

James says his friends didn't use his fame to become successful. Instead, the four friends made their own paths to success.

CASE STUDY

LEBRON AND FRIENDS

LeBron James shot to stardom while in high school. Experts called him the next great basketball star. Fans tuned in to watch his high school team play on ESPN. *Sports Illustrated* put him on the magazine's cover. The attention would be a lot for anybody, but it was especially hard on a teenager. Three close friends from his hometown of Akron, Ohio, helped James stay grounded.

James went on to become the first pick in the 2003 NBA Draft. In a career lasting more than 20 years, he proved to be an amazing player. Many consider him one of the best basketball players of all time. All the while, his three friends remained close.

Rich Paul became one of the NBA's most successful agents. James is his star client. Maverick Carter became James's business manager. One of their main business interests is a digital media company. Meanwhile, Randy Mims became James's chief of staff.

"I always knew there was something special about Randy, Rich, and Maverick and that, together, we were going to do something very different," James said in 2018. "I am so grateful and blessed that we found each other."

TIMELINE

1925

Football star Red Grange hires C. C. Pyle to negotiate his contract with the Chicago Bears. Pyle is believed to be the first sports agent.

1976

MLB players earn the right to free agency, leading to a rise in players hiring agents to represent them in contract negotiations.

1980s

An increase in cable TV usage and corporate sponsorships brings more money into sports.

2003

LeBron James enters the NBA. His friend Rich Paul goes on to become a successful agent. Another friend, Maverick Carter, eventually partners with James in a successful business career.

2022

With the help of his team at Shadow Lion, quarterback Tom Brady announces on March 13 that he is coming out of retirement to play another season with the Tampa Bay Buccaneers.

2024

On July 30, Simone Biles holds a session with her therapist hours before winning an Olympic gold medal in Paris, France.

2024

On September 3, NHL star Leon Draisaitl re-ups with the Edmonton Oilers. His new contract is worth $112 million over eight years.

2024

In December, agent Scott Boras negotiates a record 15-year contract worth $765 million for his client, baseball star Juan Soto.

GLOSSARY

client
A person who hires someone else to work for them.

contract
A legal agreement between two parties, such as a player and a team.

docuseries
A film about real-life events that is divided into multiple episodes.

draft
A system that allows teams to acquire new players coming into a league.

endorsement
A deal in which an athlete promotes a company in exchange for the company's products or money.

free agency
A professional athlete's ability to sign with any team once the athlete's contract has ended.

general manager
An executive who runs a team and is responsible for finding and signing players.

leverage
Power in a negotiation to shape the final deal in one's favor.

psychologist
A person who specializes in the study of the mind and helps patients work through mental health problems.

publicity
Attention from the media.

reputation
The way somebody is known by others.

retire
To end one's career.

re-up
To sign again with the same team.

salary cap
A limit on the amount of money that teams can pay players.

MORE INFORMATION

BOOKS

Illustrated Sports Encyclopedia. DK, 2023.

Schad, Tom. *Managing the Money: Athlete Contracts and Salary Caps*. Abdo, 2026.

Sports Superstars: LeBron James. World Book, 2024.

ONLINE RESOURCES

To learn more about people who work behind the scenes with athletes, please visit **abdobooklinks.com** or scan this QR code. These links are routinely monitored and updated to provide the most current information available.

INDEX

ABOUT THE AUTHOR

Chrös McDougall is a sportswriter, author, and book editor. He lives in Minneapolis, Minnesota, with an entourage that includes his wife, two kids, and a sleepy boxer named Eira.